The Key Facts™ on Colombia

Essential Information on Colombia

By Patrick W. Nee

The Internationalist®
www.internationalist.com

The Internationalist®

International Business, Investment, and Travel

Published by:

The Internationalist Publishing Company

96 Walter Street/ Suite 200

Boston, MA 02131, USA

Tel: 617-354-7722

www.internationalist.com

PN@internationalist.com

The Internationalist is a Registered Trademark. "Key Facts" and "The Internationalist Business Guides" are Trademarks of The Internationalist Publishing Company.

All Rights are reserved under International, Pan-American, and Pan-Asian Conventions. No part of this book may be reproduced in any form without the written permission of the publisher. All rights vigorously enforced

Table Of Contents

Chapter 1: Background

Chapter 2: Geography

Chapter 3: People and Society

Chapter 4: Government and Key Leaders

Chapter 5: Economy

Chapter 6: Energy

Chapter 7: Communications

Chapter 8: Transportation

Chapter 9: Military

Chapter 10: Transnational Issues

Map of Colombia

Chapter 1: Background

Colombia was one of the three countries that emerged from the collapse of Gran Colombia in 1830 (the others are Ecuador and Venezuela). A nearly five-decade long conflict between government forces and anti-government insurgent groups, principally the Revolutionary Armed Forces of Colombia (FARC) heavily funded by the drug trade, escalated during the 1990s. More than 31,000 former paramilitaries had demobilized by the end of 2006 and the United Self Defense Forces of Colombia as a formal organization had ceased to function. In the wake of the paramilitary demobilization, emerging criminal groups arose, whose members include some former paramilitaries. The insurgents lack the military or popular support necessary to overthrow the government, but continue attacks against civilians. Large areas of the countryside are under guerrilla influence or are contested by security forces. In October 2012, the Colombian Government started formal peace negotiations with the FARC aimed at reaching a definitive bilateral ceasefire and incorporating demobilized FARC members into mainstream society and politics. The Colombian Government has stepped up efforts to reassert government control throughout the country, and now has a presence in every one of its administrative departments. Despite decades of internal conflict and drug related security challenges, Colombia maintains relatively strong democratic institutions characterized by peaceful, transparent elections and the protection of civil liberties.

Chapter 2: Geography

Location:

Northern South America, bordering the Caribbean Sea, between Panama and Venezuela, and bordering the North Pacific Ocean, between Ecuador and Panama

Geographic coordinates:

4 00 N, 72 00 W

Map references:

South America

Area:

total: 1,138,910 sq km

country comparison to the world: 26

land: 1,038,700 sq km

water: 100,210 sq km

Area - comparative:

slightly less than twice the size of Texas

Land boundaries:

total: 6,309 km

border countries: Brazil 1,644 km, Ecuador 590 km, Panama 225 km, Peru 1,800 km, Venezuela 2,050 km

Coastline:

> 3,208 km (Caribbean Sea 1,760 km, North Pacific Ocean 1,448 km)

Maritime claims:

> territorial sea: 12 nm
>
> exclusive economic zone: 200 nm
>
> continental shelf: 200 m or to the depth of exploration

Climate:

> Tropical along coast and eastern plains; cooler in highlands

Terrain:

> Flat coastal lowlands, central highlands, high Andes Mountains, eastern lowland plains (Llanos)

Elevation extremes:

> lowest point: Pacific Ocean 0 m
>
> highest point: Pico Cristobal Colon 5,775 m

Natural resources:

> Petroleum, natural gas, coal, iron ore, nickel, gold, copper, emeralds, hydropower

Land use:

> arable land: 1.84%
>
> permanent crops: 1.66%
>
> other: 96.5% (2011)

Irrigated land:

10,870 sq km (2011)

Total renewable water resources:

2,132 cu km (2011)

Freshwater withdrawal (domestic/industrial/agricultural):

total: 12.65 cu km/yr (55%/4%/41%)

per capita: 308 cu m/yr (2010)

Natural hazards:

highlands subject to volcanic eruptions; occasional earthquakes; periodic droughts
volcanism: Galeras (elev. 4,276 m) is one of Colombia's most active volcanoes, having erupted in 2009 and 2010 causing major evacuations; it has been deemed a Decade Volcano by the International Association of Volcanology and Chemistry of the Earth's Interior, worthy of study due to its explosive history and close proximity to human populations; Nevado del Ruiz (elev. 5,321 m), 129 km (80 mi) west of Bogota, erupted in 1985 producing lahars that killed 23,000 people; the volcano last erupted in 1991; additionally, after 500 years of dormancy, Nevado del Huila reawakened in 2007 and has experienced frequent eruptions since then; other historically active volcanoes include Cumbal, Dona Juana, Nevado del Tolima, and Purace

Environment - current issues:
> Deforestation; soil and water quality damage from overuse of pesticides; air pollution, especially in Bogota, from vehicle emissions

Environment - international agreements:
> party to: Antarctic Treaty, Biodiversity, Climate Change, Climate Change-Kyoto Protocol, Desertification, Endangered Species, Hazardous Wastes, Marine Life Conservation, Ozone Layer Protection, Ship Pollution, Tropical Timber 83, Tropical Timber 94, Wetlands
>
> signed, but not ratified: Law of the Sea

Geography - note:
> Only South American country with coastlines on both the North Pacific Ocean and Caribbean Sea

Chapter 3: People and Society

Nationality:
> noun: Colombian(s)
> adjective: Colombian

Ethnic groups:
> mestizo 58%, white 20%, mulatto 14%, black 4%, mixed black-Amerindian 3%, Amerindian 1%

Languages:
> Spanish (officail)

Religions:
> Roman Catholic 90%, other 10%

Population:
> 45,745,783 (July 2013 est.)
> country comparison to the world: 30

Age structure:
> 0-14 years: 25.8% (male 6,032,725/female 5,755,437)
> 15-24 years: 18.2% (male 4,241,621/female 4,101,552)
> 25-54 years: 41.5% (male 9,376,745/female 9,597,744)

55-64 years: 8% (male 1,705,451/female 1,962,606)

65 years and over: 6.5% (male 1,242,980/female 1,728,922) (2013 est.)

Median age:

total: 28.6 years

male: 27.6 years

female: 29.5 years (2013 est.)

Population growth rate:

1.1% (2013 est.)

country comparison to the world: 108

Birth rate:

16.98/1,000 population (2013 est.)

country comparison to the world: 178

Death rate:

5.33/1,000 population (2013 est.)

country comparison to the world: 178

Net migration rate:

-0.66 migrant(s)/1,000 population (2013 est.)

country comparison to the world: 142

Urbanization:

urban population: 75% of total population (2010)

rate of urbanization: 1.7% annual rate of change (2010-15 est.)

Major cities - population:

BOGOTA (capital) 8.744 million; Medellin 3.497 million; Cali 2.352 million; Barranquilla 1.836 million; Bucaramanga 1.065 million (2011)

Sex ratio:

at birth: 1.06 male(s)/female

0-14 years: 1.05 male(s)/female

15-24 years: 1.03 male(s)/female

25-54 years: 0.98 male(s)/female

55-64 years: 0.86 male(s)/female

65 years and over: 0.72 male(s)/female

total population: 0.98 male(s)/female (2013 est.)

Maternal mortality rate:

92 deaths/100,000 live births (2010)

country comparison to the world: 81

Infant mortality rate:

total: 15.46 deaths/1,000 live births

country comparison to the world: 106

male: 18.77 deaths/1,000 live births

female: 11.96 deaths/1,000 live births (2013 est.)

Life expectancy at birth:
>total population: 75.02 years
>country comparison to the world: 99
>male: 71.82 years
>female: 78.42 years (2013 est.)

Total fertility rate:
>12.1 children born/woman (2013 est.)
>country comparison to the world: 111

Health expenditures:
>6.1% of GDP (2011)
>country comparison to the world: 106

Physicians density:
>1.47 physicians/1,000 population (2010)

Hospital bed density:
>1.4 beds/1,000 population (2011)

Drinking water source:
>improved:
>>*urban*: 99.6% of population
>>*rural*: 72.5% of population
>>*total*: 92.9% of population

unimproved:

  urban: 0.4% of population

  rural: 27.5% of population

  total: 7.1% of population (2010 est.)

Sanitation facility access:

  improved:

  urban: 82.3% of population

  rural: 65.4% of population

  total: 78.1% of population

  unimproved:

  urban: 17.7% of population

  rural: 34.6% of population

  total: 21.9% of population (2011 est.)

HIV/AIDS - adult prevalence rate:

  0.5% (2009 est.)

  country comparison to the world: 66

HIV/AIDS - people living with HIV/AIDS:

  160,000 (2009 est.)

  country comparison to the world: 32

HIV/AIDS - deaths:

  14,000 (2009 est.)

  country comparison to the world: 20

Major infectious diseases:
>degree of risk: high
>
>food or waterborne diseases: bacterial diarrhea
>
>vectorborne diseases: dengue fever, malaria, and yellow fever (2013)

Obesity - adult prevalence rate:
>17.3% (2008)
>
>country comparison to the world: 112

Education expenditures:
>4.5% of GDP (2011)
>
>country comparison to the world: 93

Literacy:
>definition: age 15 and over can read and write
>
>total population: 93.6%
>
>male: 93.5%
>
>female: 93.7% (2011 est.)

School life expectancy (primary to tertiary education):
>total: 14 years
>
>male: 13 years
>
>female: 14 years (2011)

Unemployment, youth ages 15-24:
    total: 23%
    country comparison to the world: 43
    male: 18.2%
    female: 29.9% (2008)

Chapter 4: Government and Key Leaders

Country name:
> conventional long form: Republic of Colombia
> conventional short form: Colombia
> local long form: Republica de Colombia
> local short form: Colombia

Government type:
> Republic; executive branch dominates government structure

Capital:
> name: Bogota
> geographic coordinates: 4 36 N, 74 05 W
> time difference: UTC-5 (same time as Washington, DC during Standard Time)

Administrative divisions:
> 32 departments (departamentos, singular - departamento) and 1 capital district* (distrito capital); Amazonas, Antioquia, Arauca, Atlantico, Bogota*, Bolivar, Boyaca, Caldas, Caqueta, Casanare, Cauca, Cesar, Choco, Cordoba, Cundinamarca, Guainia, Guaviare, Huila, La Guajira, Magdalena, Meta, Narino, Norte de Santander, Putumayo, Quindio,

Risaralda, Archipielago de San Andres, Providencia y Santa Catalina (colloquially San Andres y Providencia), Santander, Sucre, Tolima, Valle del Cauca, Vaupes, Vichada

Independence:

20 July 1810 (from Spain)

National holiday:

Independence Day, 20 July (1810)

Constitution:

Several previous; latest promulgated 5 July 1991; amended many times, last in 2011 (2013)

Legal system:

Civil law system influenced by the Spanish and French civil codes

International law organization participation:

Has not submitted an ICJ jurisdiction declaration; accepts ICCt jurisdiction

Suffrage:

18 years of age; universal

Executive branch:

chief of state: President Juan Manuel SANTOS Calderon (since 7 August 2010); Vice President Angelino GARZON (since 7 August 2010); note - the president is both the chief of state and head of government

head of government: President Juan Manuel SANTOS Calderon (since 7 August 2010); Vice President Angelino GARZON (since 7 August 2010)

cabinet: Cabinet appointed by the president

elections: president and vice president elected by popular vote for a four-year term (eligible for a second term); election last held on 30 May 2010 with a runoff election 20 June 2010 (next to be held in May 2014)

election results: Juan Manuel SANTOS Calderon elected president in runoff election; percent of vote - Juan Manuel SANTOS Calderon 69.06%, Antanas MOCKUS 27.52%

Legislative branch:

bicameral Congress or Congreso consists of the Senate or Senado (102 seats; members elected by popular vote to serve four-year terms) and the Chamber of Representatives or Camara de Representantes (166 seats; members elected by popular vote to serve four-year terms)

elections: Senate - last held on 14 March 2010 (next to be held in March 2014); Chamber of Representatives - last held on 14 March 2010 (next to be held in March 2014)

election results: Senate - percent of vote by party - NA; seats by party - U Party 28, PC 22, PL 17, PIN 9, CR 8, PDA 8, Green Party 5, other parties 5; Chamber of Representatives - percent of vote by party - NA; seats by party - U Party 47, PC 38, PL 37, CR 15, PIN 12, PDA 4, Green Party 3, other parties 10; note - as of 1 January 2011, the Senate currently has 101 seats after one seat became vacant due to a PL senator losing his seat for illegal collusion with the FARC; the Chamber of Representatives also has one seat vacant after only 165 of the 166 candidates were credentialed

Judicial branch:

Highest court(s): Supreme Court of Justice or Corte Suprema de Justicia (consists of the Civil-Agrarian and Labor Chambers each with 7 judges, and the Penal Chamber with 9 judges); Constitutional Court (consists of 9 magistrates); Council of State (consists of 27 magistrates)

Judge selection and term of offfice: Supreme Court judges appointed by the Congress from candidates submitted by the president; judges appointed for life; Constitutional Court magistrates - 3 nominated by the president, 3 by the Supreme Court, and 3 elected by the Senate; judges elected for individual 2-8 year terms

subordinate courts: Superior Tribunals (appellate courts for each of the judicial districts); regional courts; civil municipal courts; Superior Military Tribunal; first instance administrative courts

Political parties and leaders:

Alternative Democratic Pole or PDA [Clara LOPEZ]
Conservative Party or PC [Efrain CEPEDA Sarabia]
Green Party [Jorge LONDONO Ulloa; Enrique PENALOSA]
Liberal Party or PL [Simon GAVIRIA Munoz]
National Integration Party or PIN [Angel ALIRIO Moreno]
Radical Change or CR [Antonio GUERRA de la Espriella]
Social National Unity Party or U Party [Juan Francisco LOZANO Ramirez]

Political pressure groups and leaders:

Central Union of Workers or CUT
Colombian Confederation of Workers or CTC
General Confederation of Workers or CGT
National Liberation Army or ELN
Revolutionary Armed Forces of Colombia or FARC

International organization participation:

BCIE, BIS, CAN, Caricom (observer), CD, CDB, CELAC, FAO, G-3, G-24, G-77, IADB, IAEA, IBRD, ICAO, ICC (national committees), ICRM, IDA, IFAD, IFC, IFRCS, IHO, ILO, IMF, IMO, IMSO, Interpol, IOC, IOM, IPU, ISO, ITSO, ITU, ITUC (NGOs), LAES, LAIA, Mercosur (associate), MIGA,

NAM, OAS, OPANAL, OPCW, PCA, UN, UNASUR, UNCTAD, UNESCO, UNHCR, UNIDO, Union Latina, UNSC (temporary), UNWTO, UPU, WCO, WFTU (NGOs), WHO, WIPO, WMO, WTO

Diplomatic representation in the US:

chief of mission: Ambassador Luis Carlos VILLEGAS Echeverri (since 3 December 2013)

chancery: 2118 Leroy Place NW, Washington, DC 20008

telephone: [1] (202) 387-8338

FAX: [1] (202) 232-8643

Diplomatic representation from the US:

chief of mission: Ambassador (vacant); Charge d'Affaires Benjamin ZIFF

embassy: Calle 24 Bis No. 48-50, Bogota, D.C.

mailing address: Carrera 45 No. 24B-27, Bogota, D.C.

telephone: [57] (1) 275-2000

FAX: [57] (1) 275-4600

Key Leaders:
Pres.: Juan Manuel SANTOS Calderon
Vice Pres.: Angelino GARZON
Min. of Agriculture & Rural Development: Ruben Dario LIZARRALDE Montoya
Min. of Commerce, Industry, & Tourism: Santiago ROJAS Arroyo
Min. of Culture: Mariana GARCES Cordoba
Min. of Defense: Juan Carlos PINZON Bueno
Min. of Education: Maria Fernanda CAMPO Saavedra
Min. of Energy & Mines: Amylkar ACOSTA Medina
Min. of the Environment & Sustainable Development: Luz Helena SARMIENTO
Min. of Finance & Public Credit: Mauricio CARDENAS Santa Maria
Min. of Foreign Relations: Maria Angela HOLGUIN Cuellar
Min. of Health: Alejandro GARVIRIA Uribe
Min. of Housing & Territorial Development: Luis Felipe HENAO Cardona
Min. of Information Technology & Communication: Diego MOLANO Vega
Min. of Interior: Aurelio IRAGORRI Valencia
Min. of Justice: Alfonso GOMEZ Mendez

Min. of Labor: Rafael PARDO Rueda
Min. of Social Protection: Mauricio SANTAMARIA Salamanca
Min. of Transportation: Cecilia ALVAREZ-CORREA Glen
Dir., National Planning Dept.: Tatyana OROZCO
Prosecutor Gen.: Eduardo MONTEALEGRE Lynett
Pres., Bank of the Republic: Jose Dario URIBE Escobar
Ambassador to the US: Luis Carlos VILLEGAS Echeverri
Permanent Representative to the UN, New York: Nestor OSORIO Londono
Flag description:
> three horizontal bands of yellow (top, double-width), blue, and red; the flag retains the three main colors of the banner of Gran Colombia, the short-lived South American republic that broke up in 1830; various interpretations of the colors exist and include: yellow for the gold in Colombia's land, blue for the seas on its shores, and red for the blood spilled in attaining freedom; alternatively, the colors have been described as representing more elemental concepts such as sovereignty and justice (yellow), loyalty and vigilance (blue),

and valor and generosity (red); or simply the principles of liberty, equality, and fraternity

National symbol(s):

Andean condor

National anthem:

name: "Himno Nacional de la Republica de Colombia" (National Anthem of the Republic of Colombia)

Chapter 5: Economy

Economy - overview:
Colombia's consistently sound economic policies and aggressive promotion of free trade agreements in recent years have bolstered its ability to face external shocks. Real GDP has grown more than 4% per year for the past three years, continuing almost a decade of strong economic performance. All three major ratings agencies have upgraded Colombia's government debt to investment grade. Nevertheless, Colombia depends heavily on oil exports, making it vulnerable to a drop in oil prices. Economic development is stymied by inadequate infrastructure, weakened further by recent flooding. Moreover, the unemployment rate of 10.3% in 2012 is still one of Latin America's highest. The SANTOS Administration's foreign policy has focused on bolstering Colombia's commercial ties and boosting investment at home. The US-Colombia Free Trade Agreement (FTA) was ratified by the US Congress in October 2011 and implemented in 2012. Colombia has signed or is negotiating FTAs with a number of other countries, including Canada, Chile, Mexico,

Switzerland, the EU, Venezuela, South Korea, Turkey, Japan, China, Costa Rica, Panama, and Israel. Foreign direct investment - notably in the oil and gas sectors - reached a record $10 billion in 2008 but dropped to $7.2 billion in 2009, before beginning to recover in 2010, and reached a record high of nearly $16 billion in 2012. Colombia is the third largest Latin American exporter of oil to the United States, and the United States' largest source of imported coal. Inequality, underemployment, and narcotrafficking remain significant challenges, and Colombia's infrastructure requires major improvements to sustain economic expansion.

GDP (purchasing power parity):

$497.3 billion (2012 est.)

country comparison to the world: 29

$478.3 billion (2011 est.)

$448.5 billion (2010 est.)

note: data are in 2012 US dollars

GDP (official exchange rate):

$497.3 billion (2012 est.)

GDP - real growth rate:
    4% (2012 est.)

    country comparison to the world: 84

    6.6% (2011 est.)

    4% (2010 est.)

GDP - per capita (PPP):
    $10,700 (2012 est.)

    country comparison to the world: 110

    $10,400 (2011 est.)

    $9,900 (2010 est.)

    note: data are in 2012 US dollars

GDP - composition by sector:
    agriculture: 6.5%

    industry: 37.6%

    services: 55.9% (2012 est.)

Labor force:
    23.09 million (2012 est.)

    country comparison to the world: 88

Labor force - by occupation:
    agriculture: 18%

    industry: 13%

    services: 68% (2011 est.)

Unemployment rate:

10.4% (2012 est.)

country comparison to the world: 110

10.8% (2011 est.)

Population below poverty line:

34.1%

Household income or consumption by percentage share:

lowest 10%: 0.9%

highest 10%: 44.4% (2010)

Distribution of family income - Gini index:

58.5 (2011)

country comparison to the world: 8

53.8 (1996)

Budget:

revenues: $107.8 billion

expenditures: $106.1 billion (2012 est.)

Taxes and other revenues:

29.6% of GDP (2012 est.)

country comparison to the world: 98

Budget surplus (+) or deficit (-):

0.5% of GDP (2012 est.)

country comparison to the world: 37

Public debt:

40.5% of GDP (2012 est.)

country comparison to the world: 89

42.9% of GDP (2011 est.)

Note: data cover general government debt, and includes debt instruments issued (or owned) by government entities other than the treasury; the data include treasury debt held by foreign entities; the data include debt issued by subnational entities

Inflation rate (consumer prices):

3.2% (2012 est.)

country comparison to the world: 101

3.4% (2011 est.)

Central bank discount rate:

4.75%

country comparison to the world: 72

5% (31 December 2010 est.)

Commercial bank prime lending rate:

12.6% (31 December 2012 est.)

country comparison to the world: 71

11.22% (31 December 2011 est.)

Stock of narrow money:

$41.7 billion (31 December 2012 est.)

country comparison to the world: 51

$35.45 billion (31 December 2011 est.)

Stock of broad money:

$151.2 billion (31 December 2012 est.)

country comparison to the world: 48

$119.8 billion (31 December 2011 est.)

Stock of domestic credit:

$180.7 billion (31 December 2012 est.)

country comparison to the world: 42

$139 billion (31 December 2011 est.)

Market value of publicly traded shares:

$201.3 billion (31 December 2011)

country comparison to the world: 34

$208.5 billion (31 December 2010)

$133.3 billion (31 December 2009)

Current account balance:

-12.17 billion (2012 est.)

country comparison to the world: 177

$-9.837 million (2011 est.)

Exports:

$59.85 billion (2012 est.)

country comparison to the world: 55

$56.68 billion (2011 est.)

Exports - commodities:

Petroleum, coal, emeralds, coffee, nickel, cut flowers, bananas, apparel

Exports - partners:

US 36.6%, China 5.5%, Spain 4.8%, Panama 4.7%, Venezuela 4.4%, Netherlands 4.1% (2012)

Imports:

$54.64 billion (2012 est.)

country comparison to the world: 51

$50.52 billion (2011 est.)

Imports - commodities:

Industrial equipment, transportation equipment, consumer goods, chemicals, paper products, fuels, electricity

Imports - partners:

US 24.2%, China 16.3%, Mexico 10.9%, Brazil 4.8% (2012)

Reserves of foreign exchange and gold:

$37 billion (31 December 2012 est.)

country comparison to the world: 47

$31.91 billion (31 December 2011 est.)

Debt - external:

$80.72 billion (31 December 2012 est.)

country comparison to the world: 52

$76.92 billion (31 December 2011 est.)

Stock of direct foreign investment - at home:

$111.7 billion (31 December 2012 est.)

country comparison to the world: 37

$95.61 billion (31 December 2011 est.)

Stock of direct foreign investment - abroad:

$31.65 billion (31 December 2012 est.)

country comparison to the world: 41

$31.96 billion (31 December 2011 est.)

Exchange rates:

Colombian pesos (COP) per US dollar -

1,798 (2012 est.)
1,848 (2011 est.)
1,898.6 (2010 est.)
2,157.6 (2009)
2,243.6 (2008)

Chapter 6: Energy

Electricity - production:

63.65 billion kWh (2010 est.)

country comparison to the world: 42

Electricity - consumption:

45.35 billion kWh (2010 est.)

country comparison to the world: 49

Electricity - exports:

1.294 billion kWh (2011 est.)

country comparison to the world: 52

Electricity - imports:

8.22 billion kWh (2011 est.)

country comparison to the world: 28

Electricity - installed generating capacity:

13.54 million kW (2010 est.)

country comparison to the world: 49

Electricity - from fossil fuels:

32.9% of total installed capacity (2010 est.)

country comparison to the world: 175

Electricity - from nuclear fuels:

0% of total installed capacity (2010 est.)

country comparison to the world: 67

Electricity - from hydroelectric plants:
> 66.6% of total installed capacity (2010 est.)
>
> country comparison to the world: 25

Electricity - from other renewable sources:
> 0.4% of total installed capacity (2010 est.)
>
> country comparison to the world: 84

Crude oil - production:
> 969,100 bbl/day (2012 est.)
>
> country comparison to the world: 24

Crude oil - exports:
> 777,900 bbl/day (2009)
>
> country comparison to the world: 18

Crude oil - imports:
> 10 bbl/day (2011 est.)
>
> country comparison to the world: 81

Crude oil - proved reserves:
> 2.2 bbl (1 January 2013 es)
>
> country comparison to the world: 35

Refined petroleum products - production:
> 313,100 bbl/day (2010 est.)
>
> country comparison to the world: 42

Refined petroleum products - consumption:
> 287,000 bbl/day (2011 est.)
>
> country comparison to the world: 44

Refined petroleum products - exports:
>92,410 bbl/day (2010 est.)

>country comparison to the world: 70

Refined petroleum products - imports:
>49,790 bbl/day (2010 est.)

>country comparison to the world: 70

Natural gas - production:
>10.95 billion cu m (2011 est.)

>country comparison to the world: 41

Natural gas - consumption:
>9.08 billion cu m (2010 est.)

>country comparison to the world: 51

Natural gas - exports:
>2.11 cu m (2011 est.)

>country comparison to the world: 44

Natural gas - imports:
>40,290 cu m (2011 est.)

>country comparison to the world: 76

Natural gas - proved reserves:
>169.9 billion cu m (1 January 2012 es)

>country comparison to the world: 48

Carbon dioxide emissions from consumption of energy:
>71.15 million Mt (2011 est.)

>country comparison to the world: 49

Chapter 7: Communications

Telephones - main lines in use:

    6.291 million (2012)

    country comparison to the world: 27

Telephones - mobile cellular:

    49.066 million (2012)

    country comparison to the world: 29

Telephone system:

    general assessment: modern system in many respects with a nationwide microwave radio relay system, a domestic satellite system with 41 earth stations, and a fiber-optic network linking 50 cities; telecommunications sector liberalized during the 1990s; multiple providers of both fixed-line and mobile-cellular services

    domestic: fixed-line connections stand at about 15 per 100 persons; mobile cellular telephone subscribership is about 100 per 100 persons; competition among cellular service providers is resulting in falling local and international calling rates and contributing to the steep decline in the market share of fixed line services

<u>international</u>: country code - 57; multiple submarine cable systems provide links to the US, parts of the Caribbean, and Central and South America; satellite earth stations - 10 (6 Intelsat, 1 Inmarsat, 3 fully digitalized international switching centers) (2011)

Broadcast media:
combination of state-owned and privately owned broadcast media provide service; more than 500 radio stations and many national, regional, and local TV stations (2007)

Internet country code:
.co

Internet hosts:
4.41 million(2012)
<u>country comparison to the world</u>: 24

Internet users:
22.538 million (2009)
<u>country comparison to the world</u>: 18

Chapter 8: Transportation

Airports:
>836 (2013)
>
>country comparison to the world: 8

Airports - with paved runways:
>total: 121
>
>over 3,047 m: 2
>
>2,438 to 3,047 m: 9
>
>1,524 to 2,437 m: 39
>
>914 to 1,523 m: 53
>
>under 914 m: 18 (2013)

Airports - with unpaved runways:
>total: 715
>
>over 3,047 m: 2
>
>2,438 to 3,047 m: 9
>
>1,574 to 2,437 m: 39
>
>914 to 1,523 m: 53
>
>under 914 m: 18 (2013)

Heliports:
>3 (2013)

Pipelines:
>gas 4,991 km; oil 6,796 km; refined products 3,429 km (2013)

Railways:
> total: 874 km
>
> country comparison to the world: 95
>
> standard gauge: 150 km 1.435-m gauge
>
> narrow gague: 498 km 0.950-m gauge; 226 km 0.914-m gauge (2008)

Roadways:
> total: 141,374 km (2010)
>
> country comparison to the world: 34

Waterways:
> 24,725 km (18,300 km navigable; the most important waterway, the River Magdalena, of which 1,488 km is navigable, is dredged regularly to ensure the safe passage of cargo vessels and container barges) (2012)
>
> country comparison to the world: 6

Merchant marine:
> total: 12
>
> country comparison to the world: 106
>
> by type: cargo 9, chemical tanker 1, petroleum tanker 2
>
> registered in other countries: 4 (Antigua and Barbuda 1, Panama 2, Portugal 1) (2010)

Ports and terminals:

<u>Major seaports:</u> Atlantic Ocean (Caribbean) – Cartagena, Santa Marta, Turbo; Pacific Ocean - Buenaventura

Chapter 9: Military

Military branches:

National Army (Ejercito Nacional), Republic of Colombia Navy (Armada Republica de Colombia, ARC, includes Naval Aviation, Naval Infantry (Infanteria de Marina, IM), and Coast Guard), Colombian Air Force (Fuerza Aerea de Colombia, FAC) (2012)

Military service age and obligation:

18-24 years of age for compulsory and voluntary military service; service obligation is 18 months (2012)

Manpower available for military service:

males age 16-49: 11,692,647

females age 16-49: 11,727,625 (2010 est.)

Manpower fit for military service:

males age 16-49: 9.150,400

females age 16-49: 9,961,760 (2010 est.)

Manpower reaching militarily significant age annually:

male: 430,634

female: 413,974 (2010 est.)

Military expenditures:
    3.28% of GDP (2012)
    country comparison to the world: 52

Chapter 10: Transnational Issues

Disputes - international:

In December 2007, ICJ allocated San Andres, Providencia, and Santa Catalina islands to Colombia under 1928 Treaty but did not rule on 82 degrees W meridian as maritime boundary with Nicaragua; managed dispute with Venezuela over maritime boundary and Venezuelan-administered Los Monjes Islands near the Gulf of Venezuela; Colombian-organized illegal narcotics, guerrilla, and paramilitary activities penetrate all neighboring borders and have caused Colombian citizens to flee mostly into neighboring countries; Colombia, Honduras, Nicaragua, Jamaica, and the US assert various claims to Bajo Nuevo and Serranilla Bank

Refugees and internally displaced persons:

IDPs: 4.9 - 5.7 million (conflict between government and illegal armed groups and drug traffickers since 1985) (2013)

Stateless persons: 12 (2012)

Illicit drugs:

Illicit producer of coca, opium poppy, and cannabis; world's leading coca cultivator with 83,000 hectares in coca cultivation in 2011, a 17% decrease over 2010, producing a potential of 195 mt of pure cocaine; the world's largest producer of coca derivatives; supplies cocaine to nearly all of the US market and the great majority of other international drug markets; in 2012, aerial eradication dispensed herbicide to treat over 100,549 hectares combined with manual eradication of 30,486 hectares; a significant portion of narcotics proceeds are either laundered or invested in Colombia through the black market peso exchange; important supplier of heroin to the US market; opium poppy cultivation is estimated to have fallen to 1,100 hectares in 2009 while pure heroin production declined to 2.1 mt; most Colombian heroin is destined for the US market (2013)

Map of Colombia

Other Key Facts™ Titles

Key Facts on Syria

Key Facts on China

Key Facts on Qatar

Key Facts on India

Key Facts on Germany

Key Facts on Argentina

Key Facts on Russia

Key Facts on North Korea

Key Facts on Brazil

Key Facts on Italy

Key Facts on the United Arab Emirates

Key Facts on the European Union

Key Facts on Pakistan

Key Facts on Saudi Arabia

Key Facts on Cyprus

Key Facts on Iran

Key Facts on Afghanistan

Key Facts on Iraq

Key Facts on Indonesia

Key Facts on South Korea

Key Facts on France

Key Facts on the United Kingdom

Key Facts on Egypt

Key Facts on Israel

All Key Facts™ Titles are Available at

www.Amazon.com

THE INTERNATIONALIST®
2013
WWW.INTERNATIONALIST.COM

www.ingramcontent.com/pod-product-compliance
Lightning Source LLC
Chambersburg PA
CBHW071825170526
45167CB00003B/1417